Self-Care:

Reflect, Restructure, Reset, Renew

Make Actionable Changes to Prioritize Your Well-being

By Angela Russ-Ayon

Russ InVision Company
AbridgeClub.com
©2025 Russ InVision Company

The information provided in this book is for educational and informational purposes only and is not intended as a substitute for professional medical or mental health advice, diagnosis, or treatment. The author and contributors disclaim any liability for any loss, damage, or injury that may arise from the use of any information, ideas, or opinions in this book.

ISBN: 978-195862719-8
IngramSpark Publishing

A Note from the Author

I've faced more than my share of challenges—over $30,000 in perpetual debt, broken down cars, substantial investment losses, unfulfilling and toxic jobs, failed side hustles, strained friendships, the full-time care of my elderly mother, bereavement, morbid obesity, near-death from blood clots, crippling arthritis, clinical depression, incapacitating anxiety, a sickening fear of public speaking, and a stroke during my daughter's birth that has stolen my short-term memory for three decades.

But with time, persistence, and a shift in mindset, I turned things around. I raised two self-actualized, successful children, erased my debt, saved for retirement, let go of draining friendships, cultivated new ones, reinvented my career, built new and rewarding side hustles, replaced my knees, joined a gym, lost over 100 pounds, and faced my fear of public speaking head-on.

Now, I find time for myself. I am constantly working toward being the best version I can be. I give back. I've built meaningful relationships. I feel happy, healthy, and deeply grateful for what I have. You can, too.

I wrote this Self-Care book as a companion to my interactive keynote address to share the strategies that helped me rebuild my life. I hope these tools will guide and encourage you to work toward the positive mindset you desire. I wish you all the best!

Let's start by saying what self-care is not.

◊ Self-care is **not** about eliminating negative feelings. It's about managing stress and meeting your emotional needs all day, every day.

◊ It's **not** an item on your "to do" list that you will eventually get to as your list grows longer.

◊ It is **not** that one gift you give yourself occasionally, like the vacation once a year or the once a month massage.

You can have an occasional self-care experience or indulgence, but does it restore you?

How do you really feel the day you come back to work after a vacation?

Self-care is charting a course to get to where you need to be.

It is not a linear process. You won't start somewhere and get to the end. It's a journey with twists and turns every day, rather than a straight line to perfection. Sometimes you'll ride rough waves, other times you'll adjust your sails to take advantage of strong winds. Either way, you'll have to cast an anchor and rest for a while before moving forward. You don't want to drift off course, carried so far by the current that you lose sight of your destination and can't find your way back.

The self-care you need when you are depressed may not be the same self-care you need when you feel overworked or anxious.

The key is to find what helps you in different moments, whether it's rest, action, social support, giving back, or solitude.

Focusing on yourself can be difficult, but it isn't impossible. **You just have to START**.

> *"I am not afraid of storms,*
> *for I am learning how to sail my ship."*
>
> — Louisa May Alcott,
> Author of *Little Women*

Two individuals can have the exact same experience and react to it differently. One might beat themselves up, while the other takes control and action. One will celebrate the victory, while the other focuses on the mistakes he made along the way.

Shift Your Mindset

Looking at life through a positive lens doesn't mean ignoring challenges—it means choosing to focus on hope, gratitude, and what is within your control. Shifting your mindset toward what's been done well lowers stress, strengthens resilience, and leads to healthier choices.

You must start believing that **you and your life are worth the effort**. Then it becomes easier to rest, eat well, exercise, and nurture healthy connections. You begin to look forward to the changes you're making. You start to see and feel the benefits of your actions.

You are working on YOU. It may sound hokey, but positivity becomes your secret superpower for growth and happiness.

> *"Barn's burnt down*
> *— now I can see the moon."*
>
> — Mizuta Masahide,
> 17th-Century Japanese Poet and Samurai

Let Go!

It's you who are holding onto …

- [ ] those critical parents.
- [ ] that abusive relationship.
- [ ] that loveless marriage.
- [ ] that unsupportive boss.
- [ ] that incompetent staffer.
- [ ] that failed promotion.
- [ ] that disruptive child.
- [ ] that business that tanked.
- [ ] that money that's gone.
- [ ] that disloyal friend.
- [ ] that loss.

The person you are holding a grudge against is living *RENT FREE* in your mind all day, every day: sitting on your sofa, eating your food, and sleeping in your bed.

You cannot change what's happened.
You are not the person they think you are.
You are not the person they said you were.

Find a way to make actionable changes
and move on to the best parts of your life.

Prove them wrong.

You are worthy.
You should always be appreciated and respected.

Trust the chapters waiting to be written.

Why We Need Self-Care

50% of workers leave their jobs
because of physical and emotional stress.

It's one of the leading causes of healthcare issues. Stress triggers the release of cortisol, the body's stress hormone. This hormone can make the heart race, muscles tighten, and focus slip. In the brain, high cortisol levels can impair memory, decision-making, and learning.

We cause stress with...

- ...what we put in our bodies.
- ...what we put on our bodies.
- ...what we do or don't do with our bodies.
- ...what we expose our minds and bodies to.
- ...the negative things we say to ourselves.
- ...the people we associate with.
- ...the choices we make.

As you move through this stress test,
read each statement carefully and, in private,
count how many apply to you. Be honest with yourself.

- ☐ I neglect my diet.
- ☐ I don't move as much as I should.
- ☐ I'm at an unhealthy weight.
- ☐ I have health issues that affect my ability to do things.
- ☐ I have trouble sleeping.
- ☐ I use sleep aids.
- ☐ I'm always tired.
- ☐ I have a negative attitude.
- ☐ I'm depressed.
- ☐ I have headaches.
- ☐ I get sick often.
- ☐ I drink too much alcohol.
- ☐ I follow where I'm led.
- ☐ I don't like uncertainty.
- ☐ I use recreational drugs to feel better.

- ☐ I am always nervous or anxious.
- ☐ I don't like to be kept waiting.
- ☐ I get easily frustrated with people.
- ☐ I am easily angered by things that are out of my control.
- ☐ I rarely speak up for myself when I should.
- ☐ I am always critical of myself.
- ☐ I lack motivation.
- ☐ I can't seem to get anything done.
- ☐ I lack self-confidence.
- ☐ I have high or unrealistic expectations.
- ☐ I struggle with time management.

- [ ] I feel my opinion doesn't count.
- [ ] I try to do everything myself.
- [ ] I don't like to ask for help.
- [ ] I'm often criticized for the things I do.
- [ ] I worry a lot.
- [ ] I'm nervous when speaking in public.
- [ ] I'm easily embarrassed.
- [ ] I fear failure or making mistakes.
- [ ] I don't like to draw attention to myself.
- [ ] I have trouble concentrating.
- [ ] I have few supportive relationships.
- [ ] I don't have anyone to talk to.
- [ ] I feel betrayed by someone close to me.
- [ ] I can't depend on my parents.
- [ ] My family is not supportive.
- [ ] I keep everything inside.
- [ ] I am impatient.
- [ ] I put important things off until later/forever.
- [ ] I gossip, which can harm trust in my relationships.
- [ ] I spend time complaining about my past.
- [ ] I rarely, if ever, do anything for myself.
- [ ] I'm financially unstable
- [ ] I'm always too busy
- [ ] I often fall short of my goals.
- [ ] I have suffered loss.
- [ ] My life is in turmoil.
- [ ] I feel completely lost.
- [ ] I fail to find time to relax.
- [ ] I cry when I leave work.

The Results?

Just one checked box
can be the cause of severe stress.

☐ The first step to reducing stress is recognizing what's truly causing tension in your life. Awareness is the first step to taking back control.

☐ The second is taking action to manage or remove your stressors. You can't just sit in the airport lounge waiting for your life to take off. You must buy the ticket and board the plane.

☐ The last is nurturing your well-being with self-care practices that restore you and bring you joy every day.

What keeps you sane?

If you go after what creates meaning in your life, you will be better equipped to handle the stress that comes with it.

*"If there's something that lights you up…
something that makes you come alive,
do that thing."*

— Leslie Odom Jr.,
Performer, *Hamilton* Original Cast

How Self-Care Benefits You

1. It helps you stay sharp, be more productive, think clearly, solve problems, and spark creative ideas.

2. Your mental health improves. You learn to relax, balance your emotions, and ease your mental stress.

3. Your physical health improves. You move your body more, fuel yourself with a balanced diet, and get good, consistent sleep.

4. You build strong relationships, communicate better, and practice patience.

5. You experience personal growth and build self-worth, resilience, and the confidence to handle life's challenges.

Act today in ways
that will put you in
the right place tomorrow.

> *"You don't skate
> to where the puck is.
> You skate to where it will be."*
>
> — Wayne Gretzky,
> Professional Hockey Player

Self-care is different for each person.
Our needs, emotions, and life circumstances
are constantly changing.

It does not have to cost money.
and it does not matter…

- …how smart you are.
- …how in shape you are.
- …how talented you are.
- …how good you look.
- …how much you love your job.
- …how much money you make.
- …how great your marriage is.
- …how many friends you have.
- …how supportive your family is.
- …how famous you are.
- …how many likes or followers you have.

Everyone needs self-care
to find a good work-life balance!

Because most people are fighting
some battle you know nothing about.

One of the most common excuses
for not practicing self-care is,
"I don't have time."

Make time for self-care and restoration!
After all, you make time for everything else.

The average person spends approximately...

- ...five hours a day watching TV.
- ...50 minutes a day on social
  media apps.
- ...30 minutes a day texting.
- ...one to two hours a day
  responding to emails.

In addition, they find time for gaming,
watching sports, and commuting.

Do you make time
for everything but you?

Your past may have influenced you, but it does not have to
define you. Many of us move through life repeating the
same patterns we've carried since early adulthood, making
the same choices again and again, and holding onto old
habits and patterns that negatively affect our decisions
throughout the day.

Your time has value, so cash it in! Every day is a chance to
break free, step out of damaging routines, and choose
habits that benefit, heal, and uplift instead of harm.

Gaining More Time in Your Day

When was the last time you spent
10 minutes awake and doing absolutely
nothing?

- No hygiene
- No chores
- No eating
- No TV
- No texting
- No talking
- No reading
- No working
- No exercising
- No caring for others
- No sleeping
- No scrolling

No overwhelming, difficult emotions.
No distractions.

????????

We spend more time and energy caring for everyone else
than we do taking care of ourselves and our mental health.
And when we aren't doing that, we waste time with inefficient
habits instead of taking action to make our lives active, fun,
interesting, or rewarding. We even waste time envying those
who are constantly curating joy when their lives could be
falling apart behind their ring light.

Gaining More Time in Your Day

Time is the one thing we can't make more of—but we can learn to use it differently…wisely. Since having too much to do can be paralyzing, address your challenges one step, one breath, and one choice at a time, so they are easier to overcome.

Whatever you have to make happen, begin with what you can accomplish in five minutes, then ten, then in an hour, and so on. Once you see the results, you might be inspired to dedicate an entire day to the task. But don't beat yourself up if you stop after five minutes. See each small victory as progress, let the triumphs steady your mind, and trust that you are carrying yourself closer to brighter, better days.

By shifting small habits, setting clearer priorities, and protecting your mental space, you can uncover hidden moments that add up to hours.

Remember, you're on a ladder of growth. You can't just leap to the top; the rungs you climb must be well-constructed and close together to allow each step at a steady pace.

Gaining More Time in Your Day

This section will help you recognize where your time goes and guide you toward choices that give you more freedom, focus, and balance each day.

Health & Wellness

- [ ] Plan weekly meals to avoid last-minute, time-consuming, and costly decisions.
- [ ] Prep or cook food in batches ahead of time so meals are cooked in minutes.
- [ ] Plan for leftovers. Turn last night's dinner into today's quick, healthy lunch.
- [ ] Try affordable meal-kit delivery services.
- [ ] Buy or pack ready-to-go snacks like protein bars, fruit, veggies, or trail mix for a quick refuel.
- [ ] Don't shop when you're hungry. You will want to buy and eat everything!
- [ ] Stick to a regular bedtime, wake up early, and get your workout out of the way.
- [ ] Break workouts into mini sessions. Movement doesn't have to mean an hour at the gym.
- [ ] Pick a gym with hours that fit your schedule.
- [ ] Keep a "go bag" with water, a towel, and workout gear handy.
- [ ] Listen to an audiobook or podcast or catch up on learning while walking, jogging, or cycling.
- [ ] Turn social time into movement: walk or hike with a friend.

Gaining More Time in Your Day

Home & Daily Routines

- [ ] Clean one area of the house at a time to avoid being overwhelmed. Focus on what guests will see first.
- [ ] Combine mundane chores. For example, do the dishes while the food is cooking, or vacuum while doing laundry.
- [ ] Ask for help. Share or delegate tasks and chores.
- [ ] Cut back on screen and social media time to reclaim hidden pockets of the day.
- [ ] Place charging stations in multiple locations for quick access.
- [ ] Store your belongings in designated spaces by category. Tools go in a toolbox, first aid supplies in their own bin, books on the bookshelf, and so on. This way, you don't waste time looking for them, and you don't waste money replacing what you can't find.
- [ ] Regularly put items away so they don't pile up.
- [ ] Set out clothes, pack bags, and fill water bottles the night before. Make a checklist so you don't forget anything.
- [ ] Keep essentials like your phone, keys, and wallet easily accessible, so you don't have to search for them on the way out the door.

Gaining More Time in Your Day

Work & Productivity

- [ ] Avoid overbooking yourself. Think hard before signing up for that class or project. Leave breathing room in your schedule to enjoy the moments that matter.
- [ ] Pack work essentials the night before—your laptop, presentation, briefcase, lunch, etc.
- [ ] Know how long it takes to get somewhere and do something to avoid leaving too early, showing up late, or overcommitting.
- [ ] Leave early to skip traffic, gain quiet time on arrival, and start your day calmly.
- [ ] Batch similar tasks like calls, emails, and errands together. Plan errands around your route.
- [ ] Listen to inspirational podcasts, audiobooks, or guided meditations during your commute.
- [ ] Take the bus, subway, train, or carpool.
- [ ] Move closer to work or find a job closer to home.
- [ ] File or scan important documents.
- [ ] Consistently back up important files on your devices.

Finances

- [ ] Reduce the number of bank accounts, credit cards, or bills you manage.
- [ ] Spend less time managing bills by consolidating debt onto lower-interest (APR) credit cards or loans.

Gaining More Time in Your Day

- ☐ Sign up for purchase alerts to instantly know when and where you spend money—no combing through statements or hunting down fraud.
- ☐ Turn on alerts for due dates, low balances, and big purchases so nothing catches you off guard.
- ☐ Put bills on autopay—even for the minimum—to stay on track and avoid late fees.
- ☐ Schedule automatic deposits and transfers to savings or investment accounts.
- ☐ Use lists when you shop, to get in and out quickly before buying things you don't need.

Relationships

- ☐ Schedule time on your calendar for calls or meetups just like you would a special event.
- ☐ Walk, cook, do hobbies, or exercise with a friend or coworker.
- ☐ Carpool or travel together when possible.
- ☐ Send a quick text, voice note, or video message when you don't have time to meet in person.
- ☐ Converse while driving, cleaning, or doing other mundane tasks.
- ☐ Let go of draining relationships to make space for positive ones.
- ☐ Say no instead of taking on obligations you cannot realistically manage.

Joy often hides in small, simple moments—a hot cup of tea, a kind smile, the warmth of sunlight on your face, a cool breeze on a hot day, making snow angels, the laughter of a child, cuddling in a soft blanket, or someone opening a door for you. When life feels overwhelming, slowing down to notice these little gifts can bring you comfort and peace.

Which of These Habits are Keeping You from Finding Joy?

☐ Filling your calendar with too many commitments. Basically, you cram so many seeds into the pot, there's no room for anything to grow.

☐ Keeping busy with multiple tasks all day and never giving your mind a chance to pause, reset, or focus.

☐ Procrastinating until you have so much to do that doing anything feels overwhelming.

Finding Joy

- [ ] Saying negative and mean things to yourself, out loud or in your head, like your own personal bully is constantly escorting you.

- [ ] Doomscrolling through news, social media, or pop-ups that make you feel stressed, angry, or jealous. It's like stepping into quicksand. The more you scroll, the deeper you sink.

- [ ] Comparing and measuring your worth against someone else's highlight reel, which can ultimately make you feel like a complete failure, ignoring your own winning footage.

- [ ] Turning to food for comfort rather than addressing your feelings. It's like covering the crack in the wall with fresh paint. It doesn't fix the problem underneath.

- [ ] Binge-watching, gaming, drinking, or using recreational drugs to numb your feelings instead of dealing with the sources of your stress.

- [ ] Holding your emotions in rather than processing them in a healthy way. Eventually, your emotional closet gets so full you can't close the door.

- [ ] Isolating yourself instead of seeking support and asking for help.

- [ ] Constantly worrying about money, but taking no steps to change your situation.

Finding Joy

☐ Neglecting your body by skipping meals, failing to exercise, or rarely drinking water. How can you expect your body to last a lifetime when you treat it like this?

☐ Shoveling down your food. Do you taste what you're eating? Slow down and let the food delight your senses.

☐ Sacrificing sleep to "get more done," or ignoring physical or emotional signals that you need rest. Naps are an easy way to recharge. And, you can't fully replace the benefits of the deep, restorative sleep you miss.

☐ Working so hard that you stay late, skip breaks, take work home, or never log off. At some point, it's going to catch up with you.

☐ People-pleasing by always saying yes when you want and need to say no. When are you going to put yourself first? You don't have to be there just because it's happening.

> *"Almost everything will work again if you unplug it for a few minutes, including you."*
>
> — Anne Lamott, Bestselling Novelist

If you believe, these are the moments when faith can be your most significant source of strength.

Reconnecting with your faith doesn't mean having all the answers; it means opening your heart to hope, leaning into prayer or reflection, and trusting that you are being guided even in the darkest times.

Joining religious activities or gatherings nurtures a sense of belonging and lifts feelings of isolation. Sharing your faith with others can also spark meaningful service and collaborative volunteering, bringing purpose, connection, and fulfillment to your life.

Faith offers comfort, clarity, and a reminder that struggles are not the end of your story, but stepping stones toward growth. When you return to your faith, you rediscover the courage to keep moving forward, knowing you never walk alone.

Start and **end** your day with something
that **nourishes your body and mind**:

- [ ] meditation
- [ ] napping
- [ ] planning your day
- [ ] spending time with family
- [ ] journaling
- [ ] stretching
- [ ] tranquil movement like yoga or tai chi
- [ ] relaxing music
- [ ] aromatherapy
- [ ] gardening
- [ ] a mindful stroll
- [ ] praying
- [ ] a massage
- [ ] reading something enjoyable
- [ ] a warm or chilled soothing drink

Instead of shoveling food and guzzling drinks, take small sips and tiny bites. Hold the food or drink in your mouth a little longer before you swallow, so you can taste and appreciate what you're consuming. Appreciate the flavor. Feel the texture on your tongue. Feel the warmth or chill of the drink you're holding. Be thankful. There are people in this world who would gladly eat the food you throw away.

Finding CALM

Remove your headphones and listen to the world.
Engage all of your senses. Notice people. Notice things.

Be grateful for your life, even if it isn't perfect.
You have made it this far.

- Listen to the birds chirping.
- Feel the cool blades of grass on your bare feet.
- Listen to the soft breeze or the rustling leaves.
- Smell the scent of blooming flowers or pine trees.
- Hear the wind chimes in the distance.
- Listen to the gentle rush of ocean waves, a stream, a natural or handmade fountain, or a waterfall.
- Listen to the birds.
- Squeeze the grains of sand under your toes.
- Watch the clouds change shapes as they drift by.
- Stare at the moon.
- Look for constellations or shooting stars.
- Stamp patterns or mold shapes in the snow.
- Draw, paint, color, complete a puzzle, craft, etc.
- Light a fire and absorb the warmth.

Finding CALM

- Disconnect from your cell phone, devices, and TV in the 10-15 minutes after you wake up and 10-15 minutes before bedtime.

Blue light from screens can disrupt the natural process of melatonin production, making it difficult to fall asleep.

The news and social media can often stir up anxiety. But peace begins with focusing on what you can influence, what you can control: your thoughts, your choices, and the calm you create within.

Meditation

Meditation is an accessible, mindful, drug-free treatment that enables you to enjoy reductions in...

- ...levels of anxiety.
- ...depression.
- ...negative emotions.
- ...stress.

Can you find a moment to meditate each day?
Absolutely!

You don't need a mat on the floor to meditate.
You can do so anywhere you can find peace—in the car, on a sofa, or in a dining chair. It requires complete relaxation, so not while standing.

Meditation can put you in an alpha state of mind, where you are relaxed and able to concentrate—awake, but not actively thinking. You feel like you have shifted gears from high-speed into cruise control. It's when you walk away from a challenge or problem and the solution just comes to you suddenly in your quiet moment?

How to Meditate

Take a Moment

1. Find a quiet spot. Try to block out any noise.
2. Close your eyes.
3. Clear your mind. Sweep away all thoughts and concerns.
4. Free your hands. Rest them on your thighs, palms up.
5. Focus on relaxing your muscles. Start at the muscles in your neck, consciously working your way down your body to your feet.
6. Breathe slowly in through your nose for four counts, and out through your mouth for four counts.
7. Focus only on breathing & counting.

After each intake and exhale, silently count backwards from 50 (or 100 if you have more time) to zero.

It should take approximately one minute or more to reach 10 counts. If you count from 50, you can enter an alpha state of mind in approximately 5 minutes or more.

You have just practiced self-care!

Find a time and a place to do this every day.

Self-talk is how you talk to yourself, whether out loud or in your mind—your inner critic. The voice in your head is always guiding you through situations like the running commentary of an internal GPS (Global Positioning System), giving you directions, warnings, or encouragement.

If your internal GPS is positive and supportive, it helps you remain calm and confident on the road ahead. But if it's critical or discouraging, it can make your journey stressful and full of second-guessing. You will feel lost. The good news is, if you adjust your settings, your self-talk will be more of a helpful guide than a harsh critic.

Self-Talk

When you battle with different levels of fear, rejection, loneliness, injuries, failure, loss, guilt, or shame, self-talk can guide you with clarity. What you say to yourself matters. It can either help you adapt effectively and smoothly, or make you anxious, stressed, and unable to cope. Here are some examples of self-talk on your internal GPS.

ENCOURAGING self-talk:
◊ "Only a little farther—almost there!"
◊ "Nice job staying in your lane."
◊ "Even with all the traffic, you're making progress."

POSITIVE and PROBLEM-SOLVING self-talk:
◊ "This way might take longer, but you'll get there."
◊ "You missed the turn—let's find another way."
◊ "Slow down; let's figure this out."

CRITICAL or NEGATIVE self-talk:
◊ "You always miss this exit."
◊ "How hard is it to follow simple directions?"
◊ "You'll never get there at this rate."

> *"Whether you think you can,*
> *or you think you can't,*
> *you're right."*
>
> — Henry Ford, Auto Industrialist

Self-Talk

Hearing your inner voice criticizing you at every turn can positively or negatively influence your moods, emotions, behavior, actions, and often your outcomes. The good news is you can reprogram that voice. Instead of letting negativity control you, practice saying things to yourself that encourage, reassure, and remind you that you are capable.

The question is, "Why are you speaking to yourself this way?" You wouldn't scratch yourself, then make the cut deeper.

Here are some questions to consider:

- [ ] Why do I expect myself to be perfect when nobody else is?
- [ ] What would my parent or close friends say to me in this situation?
- [ ] Would I say the same thing to someone I care about? Would I say this to a child?
- [ ] Am I trying to convince myself not to do this?
- [ ] Am I a mind-reader to know what other people think?
- [ ] How can I learn and grow from attempting?
- [ ] How will I be harmed if I take the risk?
- [ ] Why am I afraid to try?
- [ ] What's the worst that can happen?

Personal Affirmations

Affirmations are short, encouraging statements that help you achieve a more positive frame of mind. They can be said out loud or written down.

The words of others can influence how you see yourself. Perhaps your siblings, parents, or even a boss left imprints on your thinking. What you say to yourself matters now more than ever. With awareness—and sometimes support—you can reprogram your mind, so your thoughts lift you instead of holding you back. Focus on your strengths. Manifest the life you want to design.

Become a cheering section for yourself! Catch negative self-talk patterns early and consciously choose healthier, more supportive thoughts! Ask your friends and coworkers to do the same, while they hold you accountable.

- ☐ Post affirmations where you can see them.
- ☐ Set an alarm that includes affirmations.
- ☐ Surprise yourself with an affirmation.
- ☐ Surprise someone else with one.

Positive Affirmations

I can accomplish ANYTHING.	I LEARN from my mistakes.
My life has meaning!	I am ENOUGH.
Nothing can stop me.	I look GOOD!
I live like someone left the gate open.	I do not compare myself to others.
I am in CONTROL of my life.	I am worthy of RESPECT.
I will not let others LIMIT me.	No one will push my buttons.
I will seek help.	I will say NO!
I am not DEFINED by my past.	I am strong, smart, and capable.
I choose to be HAPPY.	My hard work will pay off.
I have EARNED this.	I will make myself PROUD.
I am willing to take a RISK.	I am where I'm supposed to be.

No one will look out for your mental and physical health like you will, so take personal ownership of it.

☐ Strive for adequate sleep (7-8 hours). Take naps.

☐ Find moments to rest during the day.

☐ Drink more water. Carry an insulated water bottle so you always have clean water at hand.

☐ Plan for, prep, and eat nutritious meals.

☐ Take daily vitamin supplements.

☐ Get the routine check-ups and medical care you can afford. Take advantage of nonprofit clinics, free health screenings, and vaccination offers.

☐ Stay physically active: walk, hike, swim, dance, play a sport.

◊ Establish a workout schedule or routine.

◊ Walk the talk. Take meetings and phone calls on a walk if you must.

☐ Seek physical or mental therapy. Sometimes you just can't do it alone.

Every decision you could or could not control has brought you HERE.

But every decision you make from here on can take you to new HEIGHTS.

Research shows that music can have a powerful effect on our emotions and even on the brain itself.[2] The right song can calm your nervous system, lift your mood, or give you a burst of energy when you need it most. Here are a few simple ways to use music to support your emotional well-being and create more balance in your day.

☐ Separate your songs by feelings on your playlist.

- Choose soothing songs or sound effects that help you relax and calm your nerves, like nature sounds, classical pieces, Native American flute, or soft instrumental music.

- Choose uplifting, inspirational songs that invoke positive memories and bring a smile to your face. Select a theme song for the year!

- Choose energizing songs that motivate you to get up, dance, and move to a steady beat to release tension. Don't worry about whose watching.

☐ *SING!* Singing releases endorphins, and dancing releases tension. It doesn't matter if you sing in tune or remember the lyrics.

☐ Bring out the albums and turntable.

☐ Play or learn to play an instrument.

☐ Choose sounds and music that feed your soul.

39

Compartmentalization is the practice of giving each part of your life—work, family, friendships, hobbies, and personal growth—its own compartment or space in your mind.

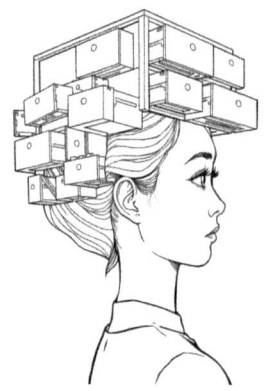

You don't have to deal with challenges all at once. Instead, place each task in its own drawer or container—real or imagined— and shut the drawer or close the lid, trusting that you'll return to it when you have the time, energy, and resources to handle it, without feeling overwhelmed.

Like any habit, controlling what your mind's focus takes practice and will strengthen with awareness. You're not ignoring your feelings—you're choosing the right time to deal with them. Adjusting your approach and making small tweaks over time will help you build mental discipline.

Compartmentalizing permits you to focus only on what's in front of you, so you can...

- ☐ ...schedule your priorities
- ☐ ...reduce stress
- ☐ ...increase your clarity and attention
- ☐ ...ensure that you're caring for yourself

- all while maintaining productivity and making progress.

How to Compartmentalize

If your car won't start at lunchtime, and you must attend a mandatory meeting at work, put the car in a compartment and focus on the meeting. There is nothing you can do about your car until the meeting is over. Ruminating over it will not only distract you and make you less productive, it will also cause you stress throughout the meeting.

Step 1 - Clarify what truly matters and what needs your attention right now. Direct your energy toward your highest priorities, and give each important task your full focus—one at a time.

Step 2 - Carve out specific and reasonable moments for what you want to accomplish. For example, when is the opportune time to deal with getting your car jumped? When can you open a compartment for five minutes of stretching and deep breathing?

Step 3 - Benefit from setting alarms or using To-Do lists and task management apps to stay on track and on time.

How to Compartmentalize

Step 4 - Set measurable, achievable goals. More than likely, you aren't going to the moon this year. You can leave prepping for that off the list for now.

Step 5 - Create appealing physical spaces.

◊ Declutter and get organized. Keeping essential items, documents, or files in order reduces stress and frees time for you to focus on other compartments.

◊ Supply your space or prepare what you need to efficiently complete the job when a compartment is open: phone numbers, passwords, account numbers, materials, tools, gear,...whatever.

◊ Store commonly used items within reach and related items together, like chargers, office supplies, ingredients, craft materials, etc.

Step 6 - Set clear boundaries

◊ Just say, "NO." Try it.

◊ Communicate with others about your availability and stick to your schedule. You made it for a reason.

◊ Avoid scheduling activities on busy days or at times that don't match your internal clock. For example, if you're not a morning person, schedule afternoon and evening appointments or meet-ups whenever possible.

Are you financially stable? If not, what steps can you take to become more secure? Because worrying about money is a massive source of stress. Why are you struggling? You may think you have exhausted all your options, but maybe  it's time to take a magnifying glass to your finances and make some tough decisions. Stop complaining and do something. What spending habits can you change? Ask yourself, "What can I do without?"

- [ ] Is your money earning interest and making *more* money for you, or is it just sitting in an account?
- [ ] Do you know how much you're spending by keeping to a budget?
- [ ] Are you trying to keep up with people who have more money than you?
- [ ] Are you living modestly or beyond your means?
- [ ] Do you spend money on nonessentials? Shop too much?
- [ ] Do you eat out too often and buy too many drinks? Consider dining and pregaming prior to an event.
- [ ] Do you spend money on essential goods and services that you could find more affordably elsewhere?
- [ ] Are you consistently transferring funds into your bank from apps like Venmo, Cash App, and PayPal, or are apps earning interest on your money?

Finding Financial Security

- [ ] Are you paying for subscriptions you don't use or need?
- [ ] Are you earning what your skills and time are worth?
- [ ] Have you asked for the promotion, raise, or bonus you've earned?
- [ ] Can you train or educate yourself to move up in your company or apply for a better-paying position?
- [ ] How about taking on a second job, even if its temporary?
- [ ] What steps are you taking to prevent AI from affecting your job security? How can you use it to your benefit?
- [ ] How can you use your expertise or skills to earn more cash? A side hustle can offer valuable tax advantages.
- [ ] Can you sell some of your clothing or belongings?
- [ ] Have you considered thrifting instead of buying new?
- [ ] Do you rely too much on credit cards to pay bills or make purchases—stuck in a cycle of accumulating interest and endless debt?
- [ ] Can you obtain a credit card with either a 0% or low-interest rate, even if for a limited time?
- [ ] How about consolidating your bills onto a low-interest credit card or loan and making larger payments?
- [ ] Can you negotiate with your creditors, the IRS, or the collection agency?

Finding Financial Security

☐ Are you benefiting from credit card, travel, dining, and other reward programs that give you points, cash back, discounts, freebies, or earned privileges?

☐ Is your car payment, parking, auto, insurance, and/or auto maintenance too high? How can you cut these costs?

☐ Is there an option to walk, take public transit, scooter, cycle, or carpool? Can you move closer to work?

☐ How can you cut the cost of your utilities? Can you snuggle into an electric blanket or conserve water?

☐ Consider tiny home living, moving to an affordable area, or moving in with family, even if temporarily?

☐ Can you take on a roommate?

☐ Are you able to rent your living space when you're absent, convert a room, park a used trailer in the driveway, or build an ADU for rental income?

☐ Can you afford to purchase a home instead of renting?

☐ Are your friends or family syphoning money from you? What would happen if you cut them off?

☐ Is your gym membership more than you can afford? How can you exercise for less, or for free?

☐ Are you prepared for a sudden job loss, health issue, or emergency by saving? What about your retirement?

Challenges are a part of being human, and it may not make a difference to you, but when you feel overwhelmed, realize that countless people are struggling quietly, in the dark, attempting to find some sun.

According to the CDC and the National Institute of Mental Health, roughly one in five adults experiences notable symptoms of depression or anxiety, and nearly one in four adults lives with some form of diagnosable mental illness. Stress—though measured differently—adds another layer, especially in the workplace.

You are not the only one carry some burden or baggage—seen or hidden. People are loaded down with trauma every day, all around you; you just can't see it.

Struggles do not define you as weak; they remind you that you're alive, growing, and learning. You don't have to carry the weight in silence—there is strength in reaching out, sharing your story, and relating to others who truly understand.

But, no one wants to hear your complaints over and over, knowing you aren't doing ANYTHING to improve your situation.

What's important is that you pack your burdens in your bags and take the necessary steps toward resolutions.

You are Not Alone

Anxiety, depression, and inner battles do not discriminate; they touch lives in every corner of the world, from quiet neighborhoods to bright stages. Even the people we admire most—actors, musicians, athletes, leaders—carry struggles behind their smiles and successes.

The difference is that many well-known figures have chosen to speak openly about their pain, reminding us that it's human to wrestle with worry, stress, sadness, or self-doubt. Their words prove that strength is not the absence of struggle—it's the courage to keep going, seek help, and believe in better days ahead.

Healing doesn't mean the damage never existed.
It means it doesn't control your life.

 "In the beginning, it was just sort of speeding and a kind of numbness and going from one thing to the next thing to the next thing. I will tell you when I realized that I thought, 'All right, if I don't calm down, I'm gonna be in serious trouble.'"
— Oprah Winfrey, Talk Show Host & Actor

*"You are not the opinion
of someone who doesn't know you."*

— Taylor Swift, Singer-Songwriter

You are Not Alone

 "I never, ever slept. Or I was sleeping at a perfect right angle—just sitting straight, constantly working at the same time," He went on to say, "The expectations were eating me alive."

— Ryan Reynolds, Actor

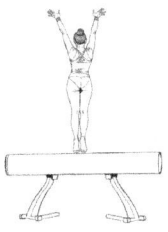

"We have to protect our body and our mind … It just sucks when you're fighting with your own head. Whenever you get in a high-stress situation, you kind of freak out. I have to focus on my mental health and not jeopardize my health and well-being."   — Simone Biles, Gold Medal Gymnast

 "I have anxiety attacks, constant panicking on stage. My heart feels like it's going to explode because I never feel like I'm going to deliver, ever, and I've thrown up a couple of times. Once in Brussels, I projectile-vomited on someone. I just gotta bear it."   — Adele, Vocalist

"It's okay to not be okay, and it's okay to talk about it. There are people who can help, and there is usually light at the end of any tunnel."
— Naomi Osaka, Tennis Pro

If You Feel Alone,
Why are You Disconnected?

Friends and relatives stop connecting with each other for a variety of reasons. Don't take it personally, unless it's personal. One or more of these may be the reason why you are disconnected from friends or family.

☐ Does work, family, health, physical activity, and daily responsibilities crowd out time for keeping in touch?

☐ Has one of you moved away, making visits and spontaneous connections harder?

☐ Are you in a stage of life, like marriage, children, or retirement, that has shifted your priorities?

☐ Have major events like divorce, financial hardship, or loss caused withdrawal? Do you think someone will judge you because of them?

☐ Have past arguments, unresolved conflicts, hurt feelings, or misunderstandings lingered, leading to endless silence, and you don't want to make the first move?

☐ Are one or both of you relying on social media "likes" and emojis instead of real conversations or meetings?

If You Feel Alone, Why are You Disconnected?

☐ Do you worry that attempts to reconnect won't be welcomed? Or the other person won't care to reconnect?

☐ Have your beliefs, political leanings, lifestyles, or goals shifted? What makes you think your true friends won't accept them?

☐ Have physical or mental health struggles made it difficult for you to reach out.

☐ Do you have a new group of friends or coworkers and aren't sure the old and the new groups will mesh? Or, maybe you fear you won't have time for both groups. You can never have too many friends, if they are the right friends.

☐ Is it that you have no idea how to restart the connection after such a long time apart?

> *"True friendship withstands time, distance, and silence."*
>
> — Isabel Allende, Chilean Author

Reasons to Reconnect
with Family or Friends

* No one else has lived those unique moments with you; revisiting them can spark joy.

* Birthdays, weddings, graduations, or even small victories are sweeter when shared.

* Old friends and family can remind you who you are and where you came from. With them, you can remove the mask, find a sense of belonging, and feel easily understood.

* Reconnection allows you to show you care and feel cared for in return.

* A fresh start can bring peace, forgiveness, and closure.

* Seeing how you've both grown can be inspiring and motivating.

* Opportunities for travel, hobbies, or simple get-togethers create new memories. Reaching out today could lead to a brighter, more connected tomorrow.

How to Reconnect
with Family or Friends

♦ **Before reaching out, reflect a bit.**

No one is perfect. Sometimes we strain relationships with the flaws we don't recognize in ourselves. You can grow and create stronger, healthier connections by asking friends and family for their perspective, embracing their feedback, and working to improve.

Think about what you hope to gain:

◊ Why do you really want to reconnect with this person? Are you seeking closure, rebuilding a bond, or simply checking in to offer aid?

◊ Is this relationship worth the time you will spend rebuilding it?

If you're seeking help, now is not the time to ask. Unless it's an emergency, people know you are only contacting them because you need or want something, and will probably feel used.

Genuine connection grows from mutual care and respect. Sometimes the best time to reconnect is when you have something to share, support, or offer in return. Then your relationship is built on balance, not just personal or professional needs.

53

How to Reconnect with Family or Friends

♦ **Start small** by leaving a short voice mail, or sending a text, email, or social media message. Something simple like, "I've been thinking of you. How are you?" Please don't assume they got your message and then get upset. Try one more time, or try communicating differently.

These days, it's easy for people to miss a message they aren't expecting. Don't take delays personally.

◊ Not everyone hovers over their phone.
◊ Not everyone can use their phone at work.
◊ Many of us have to wade through piles of texts, posts, and SPAM daily to get to the good stuff.

♦ Speak up, **clear the air**, and be honest about what was said or done. Apologize or accept the apology. Don't hold grudges. Sweep them away. A fresh start can bring peace, forgiveness, and closure. If things don't go your way, at least you made the attempt.

♦ **Be up front** about the time that's passed with a gentle acknowledgement without focusing too much on the reason or your guilt.

How to Reconnect
with Family or Friends

♦ **Share a memory,** a happy or meaningful moment you had together. It's a warm way to rekindle a connection and remind them of your bond.

♦ **Be patient.** Rebuilding trust or closeness may take time. Allow the relationship to grow naturally without forcing it.

♦ **Suggest an easy next step**, like meeting for coffee, a video call, or even exchanging updates over email, so reconnecting feels manageable. Set a date and a time, then be flexible when plans change.

♦ **Seek to solve your problems** rather than putting them on repeat for weeks, months, and years. No friend with half a brain wants to hear you recycle issues you never do anything about. Especially when they know there are solutions. Progress beats pity every time!

Do You Really Need to Reconnect?

Sometimes you just have to walk away from a relationship. Old friendships are often heavily influenced by forced physical and social proximity, like attending school, living in a small community, participating in a sport, or working on a long-term project together. In these cases, we develop friendships from a limited pool of people, regardless of our compatibility. But the pillars supporting those relationships begin to crumble once we are older, farther apart, or the seasons end.

The question is, would you choose those same friends again under different circumstances?

People come into your life for a limited time at a specific stage for a reason. They enter your life in Act 1, read their lines, and go. You can't hold onto them in Act 2 because, beyond that, there is no real connection.

We are all characters in each other's life play. So much so that you can meet someone by chance who says exactly what you need to hear at just the right moment, and then they're gone?

Whether you become friends with someone for a moment or a lifetime, there are no accidents or coincidences. You were meant to meet them, no matter how long it is. What you learn from the connection is up to you, but always welcome new friendships in different areas of your life. They will help you grow.

56

Don't expect every relationship to last forever because some won't. Be thankful for the time you had and receptive to the lesson you were meant to learn.

You should have a better understanding of who you are now.

Be more deliberate about who you befriend moving forward. Seek people who align with your sense of self and the future you're building. Look for friends who share your values and interests, like hobbies, sports, games, shows and movies, church, politics, or volunteer work, in places where you can intentionally create positive conditions for repeated interaction.

Give your best to your friends—100%, but don't overextend yourself for someone who isn't meeting you where *YOU* are. If you're starting to feel like your good nature is being habitually taken advantage of, give less, and meet them where *THEY* are. Give proportionately to what you receive and increase the percentage as they do. Doing this helps prevent feelings of resentment. Just remember to show grace when a friend is struggling.

> *"How lucky I am to have something that makes saying goodbye so hard."*
>
> — A.A. Milne,
> Author of *Winnie the Pooh*

How to Make New Connections

Research shows that making meaningful connections can positively impact your overall health.[1] So, cultivate healthy and trusting relationships with your family, friends, peers, associates, teammates, or professional network.

☐ Go somewhere. Do something new. Step out of your comfort zone. You won't hear opportunity knocking if you aren't anywhere near the door.

☐ Engage with people who support your work, mission, dream, or vision constructively—those with practical ideas and sound advice—even the advice you don't want to hear. Reciprocate.

☐ Choose people you respect and who respect you. Select kind, considerate people who give as much as they take from you.

☐ Delete unsupportive, negative, toxic friends. Just like you delete the apps that take up space and drain the battery on your phone, free up space for people who lift you higher.

☐ Schedule time to connect, just like you would any other appointment.

☐ Actively listen and be present.

☐ Speak the facts about what you're feeling in a constructive way.

☐ Argue or disagree in a "give and take" manner. In the end, you may have to agree to disagree.

☐ Stay informed. Remember what is happening in others' lives. Ask for updates. Offer help. Show you care!

How to Make New Connections

☐ Lower your expectations. Don't expect…

    …friends to change their habits, personality, or priorities to fit your needs.

    …friends to know what you want or need. They aren't mind readers.

    …equal efforts, gifts, or reciprocal gestures.

    …friends to manage the bulk of the planning, reminders, or ideas.

    …friends to spend money or time on things they aren't interested in.

    …perfection.

☐ Set boundaries and stick to them. For instance—

- Insist people treat and speak to you respectfully.
- Turn off work notifications after a specific time.
- Set aside a day to yourself to recharge.
- Don't lend money if you feel uneasy doing so.
- Don't finish the work someone else neglected.
- Hang a sign on your front door that reads, "Please call or text before knocking?"

☐ Maintain calm, and be aware of your reactions, expressions, and body language. Are you *projecting* feelings that are different than what you're saying?

☐ Work to improve yourself. Invite friends and relatives to share honestly about how you can be better. Actively listen.

☐ Choose to see the goodness in others, even when it's not obvious.

☐ Be honest. Show up. Be loyal. Keep secrets!

What habits would you like to change?
What do you want to try?
How will you find more joy and calm in each day?
What is working for your friends & peers?

1. Refer to the questions above and select coping strategies from the following list.
2. Ignore the strategies you are already doing, or that aren't possible now or ever.
3. From what remains, choose the most appealing strategy and begin with that one daily for a few weeks.
4. Then decide if the strategy has helped or not. If it has, add it to your daily routine permanently, and try another. Feel free to combine and/or alternate between strategies.

Daily Restorative Activities and Healthy Coping Strategies

- ☐ Take a break from technology. Delete apps that you binge on for a week or two. Test yourself. Detox. See where your mind goes.
- ☐ Avoid ruminating, criticizing, and bullying yourself. Use positive self-talk.
- ☐ Post and read positive affirmations and other intentional, encouraging statements. Share them with others.
- ☐ Seek to solve your problems and overcome your challenges. Take action! Innovate and improve what isn't working or is broken
- ☐ See failures and mistakes as learning opportunities. Celebrate them and take a bow!
- ☐ Minimize interruptions.
- ☐ Compartmentalize tasks.
- ☐ Get organized - declutter.
- ☐ Change your environment.
- ☐ Surround yourself with nature.
- ☐ Redecorate or redesign your space with colors and décor you find pleasing.
- ☐ Designate play, relaxation, and workspaces.
- ☐ Surround yourself with soft, warm light in soothing tones. Bright, harsh, fluorescent or blue LED light can overstimulate the nervous system.
- ☐ Relax in a hot shower, bath, jacuzzi, or steam room.
- ☐ Use a massage wand.

Daily Restorative Activities and Healthy Coping Strategies

- ☐ Sit by a burning fire or flowing water.
- ☐ Use aromatherapy with essential oils, pleasantly scented candles, or fresh flowers.
- ☐ Re-examine and restructure your relationships. Which are positive and which are toxic?
- ☐ Reconnect with supportive friends and family.
- ☐ Set boundaries and hold to them. Just say NO.
- ☐ Play with a child.
- ☐ Avoid foods and products that contain harmful chemicals—products such as shampoos, lotions, make-up, cleaning agents, sunscreen, etc.
- ☐ Wear and surround yourself with colors that calm and enhance your mood.
- ☐ Wear comfortable clothing made of natural fibers.
- ☐ Engage in creative activities: bake, write, draw, paint, color, doodle, mold clay, complete a puzzle, etc.
- ☐ View photos of beautiful images (guided visualization) and positive memories.
- ☐ Learn or practice a new skill, language, or talent—like playing an instrument, knitting, painting, or arranging flowers.

Daily Restorative Activities and Healthy Coping Strategies

☐ Watch movies, shows, and comedians that make you laugh.

☐ Listen to music that calms, or motivates and inspires you.

☐ Sing and dance.

☐ Move more. Get physically active. Walk!

☐ Write in a positivity or gratitude journal daily.

☐ Find something for which to be thankful.

☐ Look to your spirituality…your faith.

☐ Forgive someone.

☐ Find ways to give back. Surprise someone with a random act of kindness.

☐ Volunteer, mentor, or tutor. Share your knowledge. Visit orphans. Hold babies. Foster a child.

☐ Join an emotional support group.

☐ Consider an emotional support animal.

☐ Foster a pet.

☐ Ask for help when you need it. Seek therapy.

Close your eyes and imagine the life you long for—the places you'll go, the joy you'll feel, the person you'll become. Every dream, every goal, every step forward begins in your mind. The clearer the vision, the stronger the pull toward making it real. Visualization isn't wishful thinking; it's a powerful tool that turns "someday" into a plan for today.

Your homework is to create a **Vision Board**, a collection of images and inspirational phrases that reflect your positivity, goals, dreams, bucket list items, affirmations, and actions for self-care. Use printed images, drawings, photos, and phrases that benefit your mental, emotional, and physical health. Display your board where you can see it every day.

References

1. Wickramaratne, P. J., Yangchen, T., Lepow, L., Patra, B. G., Glicksburg, B., Talati, A., Adekkanattu, P., Ryu, E., Biernacka, J. M., Charney, A., Mann, J. J., Pathak, J., Olfson, M., & Weissman, M. M. (2022). Social connectedness as a determinant of mental health: A scoping review. PLOS ONE, 17(12), e0275004. https://doi.org/10.1371/journal.pone.0275004

    Miething, A., Almquist, Y. B., Östberg, V., & et al. (2016). Friendship networks and psychological well-being from late adolescence to young adulthood: A gender-specific structural equation modeling approach. *BMC Psychology, 4*, 34. https://doi.org/10.1186/s40359-016-0143-2

2. Hides, L., Dingle, G., Quinn, C., Stoyanov, S. R., Zelenko, O., Tjondronegoro, D., Johnson, D., Cockshaw, W., & Kavanagh, D. J. (2019). Efficacy and outcomes of a music-based emotion regulation mobile app in distressed young people: Randomized controlled trial. *JMIR mHealth and uHealth, 7*(1), e11482. https://doi.org/10.2196/11482

    Hereld, D. C. (2019). *Music as a regulator of emotion: Three case studies. Music & Medicine, Vol. 11*(3), 183-194. https://doi.org/10.47513/mmd.v11i3.644

    Huang, B., Hao, X., Long, S., Ding, R., Wang, J., Liu, Y., Guo, S., Lu, J., He, M., & Yao, D. (2021). The benefits of music listening for induced state anxiety: Behavioral and physiological evidence. *Brain Sciences, 11*(10), 1332. https://doi.org/10.3390/brainsci11101332